JULIA ROBERTS

A Real-Life Reader Biography

Wayne Wilson

Mitchell Lane Publishers, Inc.
P.O. Box 619 • Bear, Delaware 19701

Real-Life Reader Biographies

Selena	Robert Rodriguez	Mariah Carey	Rafael Palmeiro
Tommy Nuñez	Trent Dimas	Cristina Saralegui	Andres Galarraga
Oscar De La Hoya	Gloria Estefan	Jimmy Smits	Mary Joe Fernandez
Cesar Chavez	Chuck Norris	Sinbad	Paula Abdul
Vanessa Williams	Celine Dion	Mia Hamm	Sammy Sosa
Brandy	Michelle Kwan	Rosie O'Donnell	Shania Twain
Garth Brooks	Jeff Gordon	Mark McGwire	Salma Hayek
Sheila E.	Hollywood Hogan	Ricky Martin	Britney Spears
Arnold Schwarzenegger	Jennifer Lopez	Kobe Bryant	Derek Jeter
Steve Jobs	Sandra Bullock	**Julia Roberts**	Robin Williams
Jennifer Love Hewitt	Keri Russell	Sarah Michelle Gellar	Liv Tyler
Melissa Joan Hart	Drew Barrymore	Alicia Silverstone	Katie Holmes
Winona Ryder	Alyssa Milano	Freddie Prinze, Jr.	Enrique Iglesias
Christina Aguilera			

Library of Congress Cataloging-in-Publication Data
Wilson, Wayne.
    Julia Roberts / Wayne Wilson.
        p. cm.—(A Real-life reader biography)
    Includes index.
    Summary: A brief biography of the well-known actress, Julia Roberts, star of such films as "Steel Magnolias," "Pretty Woman," and "My Best Friend's Wedding."
    ISBN 1-58415-028-9
    1. Roberts, Julia, 1967—Juvenile literature. 2. Motion picture actors and actresses—United States—Biography—Juvenile literature. [1. Roberts, Julia, 1967- 2. Actors and actresses. 3. Women—Biography.] I. Title. II. Series.
PN2287.R63 W55 2000
791.43'028'092—dc21
[B]
                                                                     00-027390

ABOUT THE AUTHOR: Wayne Wilson was born and raised in Los Angeles. He received a Master of Arts in Education from the University of California, Los Angeles. For 16 years he was co-owner and president of a pioneering and innovative publishing company specializing in multicultural designs. Recently he completed interviews with influential Latino men throughout the country and wrote over 160 biographies for *Encuentros: Hombre A Hombre*, a comprehensive vocational education book to be published by the California Department of Education. Several of Wilson's short stories have been published in commercial and literary magazines. Wilson lives in Venice Beach, California with his wife and daughter and is currently working on his first novel and screenplay.

PHOTO CREDITS: cover: Globe Photos; p. 4 AP Photo; p. 7 The Kobal Collection; p. 9 Archive Photos; p. 12 Globe Photos; p. 13 The Kobal Collection; p. 14 Fotos International/Archive Photos; p. 15 Globe Photos; p. 17 Corbis; p. 21 Reuters/Corbis; p. 24 Globe Photos; p. 29 Mitch Gerber/Corbis.

Table of Contents

Chapter 1
Just a
Country Girl

Superstar Julia Roberts is the highest-paid actress in history. According to the *Los Angeles Times*, Julia is the only female star who can pull in $100 million in domestic ticket sales in movie after movie. *Entertainment Weekly*, in its annual "Power List" of heavyweights in the Hollywood industry, ranked Julia Roberts at number 8. No other female star came close. The next was Jodie Foster at number 59. In a male-dominated industry, Julia Roberts is the only actress who has been able to consistently bring

Julia's movies always bring in the audiences.

Julia is just a down-home country girl at heart.

in audiences. She can command $20 million per picture and has her own film production company. She is in such demand that she was able to turn down the female lead in the Academy Award–winning film *Shakespeare in Love* without a single regret.

Yet, despite all the glamour and all the acclaim, at heart, Julia Roberts is just a down-home country girl. She loves biscuits and gravy, goes bowling, likes to knit and do needlepoint (sometimes while on break between scenes in her movies), is an avid book reader, and owns seven dogs she rescued from the pound.

The youngest of the three children of Walter and Betty Roberts, Julie Fiona Roberts was born on October 28, 1967. She grew up in Smyrna, Georgia, a suburb of Atlanta. Julia's older brother Eric was born in 1956 and her sister Lisa was born in 1965. Her parents ran a small workshop for actors and writers in Piedmont Park, in Atlanta. However, "It was pretty much over by the time I could walk and talk and formulate my thoughts," she mentioned to *Harper's Bazaar* in 1997. In a 1990 interview with *Newsweek* she says, "My dad ended up selling vacuum cleaners and my mom got a job as a secretary. They never got rich and they never got famous, but they showed me that you do things for a purpose, and if it treats you well, then

all the better. But if it goes away, you won't die, just move on." It was her father's passion for acting that ultimately inspired Julia, Eric, and Lisa to pursue careers in acting.

It was her father's passion for acting that ultimately inspired Julia and her siblings to pursue careers in acting.

However, the early years were not easy for the auburn-haired little girl with the contagious smile. She was forced to grow up fast. Her parents divorced in 1971 when she was only four years old. After a bitter custody battle, Julia and her sister lived with her mother and Betty's second husband, Michael Motes in Smyrna, Georgia. Betty went to work as a church secretary. Eric lived with his father in Atlanta.

Julia does not have very fond childhood memories of her stepfather, who is reported to have been an angry and difficult man. Julia idolized her father, but she was rarely allowed to see him after the divorce. Nevertheless, she maintained a strong bond with him. When Julia was ten, her father died of cancer, and the loss deeply saddened her. It had a profound impact on the rest of her life. She still holds on to a letter that he wrote to her in 1977. "If anybody ever took that away from me I would just be destroyed," she told *Cosmopolitan*. "I can read that letter ten times a day, and it moves me in a different way every time."

Julia also has a few photographs from the days when her family ran the acting workshop. They remind her of the times when her family was happy and still together. She says that being on a movie set and forming new bonds gives her a sense of family. It helps her to forget about the disappointments of her childhood.

With her good looks and wide-mouthed smile, Julia is a filmgoers favorite.

Chapter 2
America's Sweetheart

At first, Julia wanted to be a veter— inarian.

In the September 1990 issue of *People Weekly*, Julia's mother says that although Lisa and Eric always wanted to become actors, "all Julie ever talked about was becoming a veterinarian." Nevertheless, three days after graduating from Campbell High School in 1985, Julia changed her mind and decided to join her siblings in New York City to pursue an acting career. She moved in with her sister, Lisa. Her first job was in a shoe store. She tried some modeling while searching for worthwhile acting roles but met with little success. During this time, Eric Roberts had carved out a successful acting career appearing in the *Pope of Greenwich Village, Star 80,* and receiving an Oscar nomination for *Runaway Train.* In 1986 he got Julia her first film role by convincing the director to cast her as his sister in the low-budget western *Blood Red* which was not released until 1989. It went straight to video. Soon after filming this movie she landed a role in the film *Satisfaction* (1988).

Next, Julia auditioned for a part in a youth-oriented picture. She was told that her reading was fantastic, but she wasn't quite right for the part. The character was supposed to be a fiery Portuguese woman, and they wanted someone with a more ethnic look. "When Julia wants something, she goes after it...to look more the part, she put black mousse in her hair for the callback the next day," recalls her agent, Elaine Goldsmith in the *Los Angeles Times.* She got that part and the 1988 sleeper *Mystic Pizza* turned out to be her breakthrough

Eric was on his way to a successful acting career when Julia decided she wanted to act, too.

Her breakthrough movie, Mystic Pizza, *provided Julia the break she needed for a successful career.*

role. She was 21 years old at the time and never looked back.

In 1989 Julia replaced Meg Ryan and appeared opposite a team of veteran actors that included Sally Field, Shirley MacLaine, Dolly Parton, Daryl Hannah, and Dylan McDermott as the doomed Shelby, a diabetic bride-to-be in the Southern melodrama *Steel Magnolias*. Her efforts were rewarded with an Oscar nomination for Best Supporting Actress and a Golden Globe Award. The film, a classic tearjerker, made Julia a star. She was soon dubbed America's Sweetheart. Her co-star Sally Fields commented to the *Times* that she definitely stood out: "Something about her makes you care for her." Her next film, *Flatliners* (1990), was a more serious drama about a medical student experimenting with life-after-death experiences.

Julia, in Steel Magnolias

The film that established her as a household name was the sentimental

Julia Roberts was propelled to superstardom when she starred with Richard Gere in Pretty Woman.

romantic comedy costarring Richard Gere called *Pretty Woman* (1990). The movie about a call girl with a heart of gold was a runaway international hit. Her box office appeal and celebrity status skyrocketed her to superstardom. During this same year she filmed her second runaway hit, the thriller *Sleeping With the Enemy*. The two films grossed a

combined $278 million, and Julia was recognized as the only female star who could "open" a picture during this time. Her asking price per movie climbed to $7 million.

Julia, with her co-star Patrick Berger, from the film Sleeping With the Enemy.

Julia's popularity was so enormous by 1991 that it was unusual to find a magazine without her picture on the cover. The movie audience had fallen in

"She's got all the qualities that people want an American woman to have," said Rupert Everett.

love with this tall (five-foot-nine), slender, and attractive young woman who radiated so much screen charisma with her wide, expressive mouth, big brown eyes, and thick mane of curly hair. To each role she brought beauty, sophistication, innocence, vulnerability, and charm. She projected a small-town, girl-next-door wholesomeness that both men and women could relate to. Rupert Everett, her friend and costar in the comedy hit *My Best Friend's Wedding,* said this to *Vanity Fair:* "She's really Miss America, isn't she? She's got all the qualities that people want an American woman to have."

Other films soon followed, including *Dying Young* (1991), *Hook* (1991), *The Player* (1992), *The Pelican Brief* (1993), *I Love Trouble* (1994), *Something to Talk About* (1995), *Mary Reilly* (1996), *Everyone Says I Love You* (1996), *Michael Collins* (1996), *Conspiracy Theory* (1997), *My Best Friend's Wedding* (1997), *Stepmom* (1998), *Notting Hill* (1999), and *Runaway Bride* (1999). In 2000, she made the film *Erin Brockovich*, a true story about a twice-divorced mother who takes on a public utility company and wins.

Julia co-starred with Cameron Diaz in My Best Friend's Wedding.

Although not all of her films were huge box office smashes, the *Los Angeles Times* reports that "20 of her top-grossing pictures have amassed a combined $1.4 billion in domestic box office receipts." Domestic receipts do not include the box office receipts from other countries. As of the year 2000, she has brought $2.3 billion into the theaters. She has also been nominated for two Oscars and won two Golden Globes.

Chapter 3
The Cost
of Fame

There is a downside to being a celebrity.

During her rise to movie stardom, Julia quickly found out that there is also a downside to being the most popular actress in Hollywood. "I don't think I realized that the cost of fame is that it's open season on every moment of your life," reflects Julia. As amazing as it may seem, instant success almost destroyed her. At the age of 21, she was not prepared for what life in the public eye would be like. Every time she stepped outside it was a media event. The paparazzi (celebrity photographers) constantly followed her, flashing lightbulbs in her face and shouting her name. Every mistake she made became a headline. Every date she had became a photo opportunity. Once it got so bad, she remembers, she scolded three tabloid photographers after they jumped out of a hedge to snap her picture: "You must be so proud! When your son says, 'Dad, what do you do?' you say, 'I jump out of bushes and terrorize women in the night!'" The intense media scrutiny forced her to battle false and painful rumors about her family, relationships, and conflicts with costars on her movie sets.

In 1991 she was engaged to actor Kiefer Sutherland. Three days before the ceremony, realizing that the match wasn't right, Julia called off the marriage. The scandal that erupted from this turn of events led to a flurry of media attention. Reporters and photographers followed her everywhere—they even dug through her trash, looking for clues to her private life.

Reporters and photo- graphers follow her every- where. It is difficult for her to have a private life.

In 1993, Julia married country music star Lyle Lovett.

Depressed and tired of all the negative publicity, Julia decided to take a break and slow down. She disappeared from the Hollywood scene and did not accept another movie role for nearly two years. (She did make a cameo appearance as herself in Robert Altman's satirical movie *The Player.*) Julia insists that she was taking time to relax and was waiting for the right scripts to come in. The entertainment press saw it differently. During her absence the media filled the void by cranking out various reports, ranging from Julia's having a nervous breakdown to her being a drug addict and anorexic. Julia was hurt and angry. It baffled her that people were so quick to believe the bad things about someone instead of the good.

Although Julia has had a rocky relationship with the press over the years, she has learned to cope with the challenges of success. She has matured into a person who is far more self-confident and in control of her life. "I think as I'm getting older, I'm getting smarter," says Julia thoughtfully. She has also gained a better sense of humor about the press and tries not to get upset over silly interviews. "You will never, ever outrun the tabloids," she concedes.

Julia with Lyle Lovett

Julia found romance again in 1993 when she married country music star Lyle Lovett. The press labeled the twosome an odd couple and considered the relationship bizarre. But Julia and Lyle didn't care. They had met through mutual friends and were instantly attracted to each other. Both were from the South, and they found they had much in common. Lyle was older and provided a stability for Julia that she had never known. Yet, after twenty-one months of marriage, Julia and Lyle divorced. They parted as good friends.

Chapter 4
Back on Top

Though several of Julia's films have not been successful, many are true box-office hits.

Julia Roberts is a person who likes to take career risks and try new things. She has been very fortunate in her film career and even though films such as *I Love Trouble* (1994), *Michael Collins* (1996), and *Mary Reilly* (1996), bombed at the box office, the adoring public continues to support her efforts and rush to the theaters whenever a Julia Roberts picture opens. But there is no debating that fans prefer to see Julia in a romantic comedy than in a serious drama. She made a triumphant return to comedy in 1997 when she starred in *My Best Friend's Wedding*. In this film she plays a character who refuses to lose her male best friend to another woman. The picture earned $21.5 million dollars on its opening weekend, which was her best opening at the time. Once again, the audience was thrilled to see her flashing her radiant smile. Another major hit at the box office was when she was reunited with her *Pretty Woman* costar and friend Richard Gere and director Garry Marshall to create the magic again in *Runaway Bride* (1999).

Ironically, the movie that most closely mirrors Julia's life is the 1999 feature *Notting Hill*. In that movie she plays Anna Scott, the biggest movie star in the world who falls in love with a bookstore owner (played by Hugh Grant) while working in London. Julia admits that at times she didn't know whether she was Julia Roberts or Anna Scott, particularly when the character was hounded by the press. Still, she is quick to point out that Anna Scott is a completely different person from her, and she does not agree with many of the

The movie that Julia played in that most closely resembles her life is *Notting Hill*.

things Anna does in the movie. "I was struggling with playing a person who really only shares an occupation and a height and a weight and a status with me," she recalls. Julia finds that Anna Scott is most like her near the end of the film when she has a stronger sense of what she wants in life and why she wants it.

Chapter 5
Family, Children, and Romance

Friendship means a lot to Julia, and so does family. She has a very close knit group of friends that she sees all the time. Julia is very devoted to her mother who still lives in Smyrna and works as a real estate agent. She considers her sister Lisa one of her best friends. She also adores her niece Emma (the daughter of Eric Roberts and Kelly Cunningham). Both her mother and her sister have appeared in small roles in her films.

Sadly, her relationship with her brother has fallen apart. The siblings, who at one time were very close,

Family and friends mean a lot to Julia.

haven't spoken to each other in years after several bitter arguments. Eric is also estranged from his mother—he had stopped speaking to her after his parents' divorce. Eric was very close to his father, who helped him overcome his stuttering problems as a child. (Walter discovered that his son spoke normally when he memorized his speeches.) Eric was deeply affected by his father's death. He also had to come to terms with his success in New York as an actor. The handsome and rebellious actor had a long battle with drug addiction, which he confesses started when he was 11 years old. However, he has managed to stay clean since he entered a 12-step recovery program. Eric believes that many of the problems between him and his family stem from their troubled childhood, where, he tells *Good Housekeeping*, "none of us got enough love." Moreover, he says, "Julie and I don't get along, but I love her. I'll always love Julie."

Julia owns a home in Hollywood Hills, California. When she needs a change of pace, she retreats to her getaway ranch house, which is surrounded by 50 acres in Taos, New Mexico. But she spends most of her time in a renovated duplex in New York that overlooks Manhattan's Gramercy Park. She finds that she is more comfortable on the streets of New York than Los Angeles because she is not surrounded by the celebrity scene. She can walk down the street and ride the subways without being bothered. She has no maids or servants and does her own laundry. "I find the more normal I make my life, the better it is," Julia says.

She is frequently seen running from her Manhattan apartment in leotards and sweats, without makeup, to her production company, Shoelace Productions, which she started in 1995. The company produced *Stepmom* in 1998. Julia was attracted to the project for two reasons: it gave her the opportunity to work with her good

Julia finds it easier to go un— noticed in New York instead of Los Angeles, where she is sur— rounded by the celebrity scene.

friend Susan Sarandon, and it was a film about kids.

Her love and concern for children led her to follow the late actress Audrey Hepburn, one of Julia's role models, in becoming involved with UNICEF (United Nations Children's Educational Fund) charities. In 1995, while on a trip to Haiti as a goodwill ambassador for UNICEF, she observed the horrid conditions of the starving and homeless children in that region. Since then she has become a dedicated advocate for children and has devoted much time to visiting different countries to promote goodwill and peace. In 1997 she also became involved in a charity started by actor Paul Newman called the Hole in the Wall Gang Camp, which is a nonprofit camp for children suffering from cancer and other serious illnesses. She participated with other actors in a play for children there.

The charming, sensitive, and cheerful Julia Roberts on the screen is the same person many of her friends

Julia loves children and she is involved with UNICEF.

declare you will find offscreen. No matter how famous she is, she still loves to knit sweaters, crochet rugs, bake bread, spend time with friends, and cook holiday meals. She is a nice, talented small-town Southern girl.

And she still has not lost faith in romance. After a number of failed relationships, it appears she has found a new love. Currently, she is dating actor Benjamin Bratt. His fans recognize him as Detective Rey Curtis on the NBC crime show *Law & Order*. In May 1999 Bratt finished his last season on the show to pursue a movie career. Julia even made a guest appearance on the show in 1999 to much fanfare.

Julia with Benjamin Bratt

Chapter 6
A Fairy-Tale Ending

There are up sides to being a celebrity, too. Julia lives a privileged life.

These days it appears that Julia Roberts has arrived at a good place in her life. She finds there are great advantages to being a celebrity: "I work when I want to work, and I work with people I want to work with. I travel to fabulous places. I'm surrounded by wonderful, interesting people. I live a privileged life. It's an excellent life. I'm rich. I'm happy. I have a great job."

In an interview with TV reporter Diane Sawyer, Julia likened her journey in life to a fairy tale: "Once upon a time there was a girl who led a happy life, filled with beautiful people and wonderful mistakes, and one day she woke up and was able to realize that."

Filmography

1986 *Crime Story* (TV series)

1987 *Firehouse* (TV movie)

1988 *Satisfaction; Baja Oklahoma, Mystic Pizza; Miami Vice* (TV series, guest role)

1989 *Steel Magnolias; Blood Red* released

1990 *Flatliners; Pretty Woman*

1991 *Sleeping With the Enemy; Dying Young; Hook*

1992 *The Player* (cameo)

1993 *The Pelican Brief*

1994 *I Love Trouble; Prêt-à-Porter (Ready to Wear); Sesame Street*

1995 *Something to Talk About; Before Your Eyes: Angelie's Secret* (TV special)

1996 *Mary Reilly; Everyone Says I Love You; Michael Collins; Friends* (TV series, guest star)

1997 *My Best Friend's Wedding; Conspiracy Theory*

1998 *Stepmom; Murphy Brown; In the Wild—Orangutans With Julia Roberts* (TV, PBS Special)

1999 *Notting Hill; Runaway Bride; Law & Order* (TV series, guest appearance)

2000 *Erin Brockovich*

Chronology

Index

J
B   Wilson, Wayne,
ROBERTS   1953-

          Julia Roberts.

$15.95   Grades 4-6

DATE			